W9-AYQ-425

Columbia University

Contributions to Education

Teachers College Series

No. 933

AMS PRESS
NEW YORK

THE RELATIONSHIP BETWEEN CONTENT OF AN ADULT INTELLIGENCE TEST AND INTELLIGENCE TEST SCORE AS A FUNCTION OF AGE

By Rose Estrin Kushner, Ph.D.

TEACHERS COLLEGE, COLUMBIA UNIVERSITY

CONTRIBUTIONS TO EDUCATION, NO. 933

BUREAU OF PUBLICATIONS

TEACHERS COLLEGE, COLUMBIA UNIVERSITY

NEW YORK, 1947

Library of Congress Cataloging in Publication Data

Kushner, Rose (Estrin) 1907-
    The relationship between content of an adult intel-
ligence test and intelligence test score as a function
of age.

    Reprint of the 1947 ed., issued in series: Teachers
College, Columbia University. Contributions to educa-
tion, no. 933.
    Originally presented as the author's thesis, Columbia.
    Bibliography: p.
    1. Age and intelligence. I. Title. II. Series:
Columbia University, Teachers College. Contributions
to education, no. 933.
BF433.A3K87 1972   153.9'3   75-176935
ISBN 0-404-55933-6

Copyright, 1947, by Rose Estrin Kushner
Reprinted by Special Arrangement with Teachers
College Press, New York, New York

From the edition of 1947, New York
First AMS edition published in 1972
Manufactured in the United States

AMS PRESS, INC.
NEW YORK, N. Y.   10003

ACKNOWLEDGMENTS

THE AUTHOR wishes to acknowledge her indebtedness to Professor Irving Lorge for his supervision of this study and his valuable suggestions and advice concerning it. She wishes to thank Dr. E. A. Nifenecker, Director of the Bureau of Reference, Research, and Statistics of the Board of Education of New York City, for permission to conduct the investigation in Public Schools 64 and 3; Dr. Henry M. Gould, Principal of Public School 64, and Miss Amy A. English, Principal of Public School 3, for their cooperation in the task of collecting data; Mrs. Lillian E. Harbater and Miss Anna Dragositz, for innumerable services which lightened the task of completing the study; and her husband, Charles G. Kushner, whose constant encouragement and patience made it all possible.

R. E. K.

CONTENTS

THE RELATIONSHIP BETWEEN
CONTENT OF AN ADULT INTELLIGENCE
TEST AND INTELLIGENCE TEST SCORE
AS A FUNCTION OF AGE

CHAPTER I

THE PROBLEM

THE INCREASING USE of intelligence tests for purposes of classification and guidance has created a need for accurate appraisal of intellectual ability at all age levels. To utilize fully the potentialities of our aging population with its lengthening life span, adequate appraisal of adult abilities is imperative. The American public is aware of the need for guidance and selection so that the tasks of the nation will be accomplished efficiently and competently with a minimum wastage of available manpower. Industry also has recognized the advantages of appraising intelligence and other abilities to make selection from applicants before they are hired. The United States armed forces in World War II, as in the first World War, resorted to paper-and-pencil general classification tests for the appraisal of over ten million men. The evaluation of adult intellect has become so widespread that in nearly every phase of American life today intelligence and other ability tests are used.

Under the impetus given the use of adult intelligence tests during the past decade, there is greater need to evaluate critically adult intelligence tests. Generally, an intelligence test is made up of items involving such tasks as successful performance with vocabulary, arithmetic, synonym, antonym, proverbs, analogies, and other items partaking of performances closely related to academic achievement. Usually a variety of such items involving different contents are included within a single testing instrument and the sum of credits earned, regardless of the kind of task, is considered as a score indicative of general intelligence.

Some varieties of test content appear to become increasingly difficult for progressive age groups. Measures of differential decline among different subtests of content have been based, in the main, on conclusions drawn from comparison of mean content subtest scores of different age groups. Jones and Conrad [11]* have shown that on the Group Examination Alpha (Army Alpha test), given to 1,191 subjects between the ages of 10 and 60, scores on the subtests of vocabulary and of information did not decline with increasing age. On the subtests of analogies, of common sense, and of numerical completion (which they consider best for the measurement of basic intelligence) the scores declined most rapidly with increasing age. They infer that the differential decline is attributable to the waning of intellectual powers with increasing age, and that the decline in intellectual ability is revealed more dramatically by some contents than by others.

The analysis by Jones and Conrad was based on the mean score of each content subtest on the Army Alpha test plotted according to ten-year intervals. Factors such as schooling, motivation, and speed that may be associated with decline were considered unimportant or inoperative by the investigators. The Army Alpha test, it should be noted, consists of contents chosen primarily for the purpose of arousing interest in the people whom it was intended to appraise, that is, military personnel, and not civilians. Yoakum and Yerkes[1] state that Army Alpha is applicable only within certain limits to other groups than that for which it was prepared. The test was standardized on men in the regular Army and the National Guard, as well as members of officers' training schools and students in colleges and universities. The standardization age range, therefore, did not sample the upper age brackets, so that the inference of decline in performance with certain contents is based on comparisons with performances of younger age groups for whom such content was originally intended. Moreover, each of the content subtests of the test has been shown to be approximately equally valid measures of intelligence.[2] Correlations with the

---

* Numbers in brackets refer to numbered items in Bibliography, pp. 57 to 59.
[1] C. S. Yoakum and R. M. Yerkes, *Army Mental Tests.* Henry Holt and Co., New York, 1920.

Stanford Revision of the Binet-Simon Test (1916 revision) are as follows: Oral Direction .66; Arithmetical Reasoning .73; Practical Judgment .77; Synonym-Antonym .75; Disarranged Sentences .71; Number Series Completion .25; Analogies .82; Information .73. With the exception of Number Series Completion, each of the content subtests provides an equally adequate measure of intelligence against a standard criterion of general intelligence. The intelligence ratings by officers based on a five-point scale of 672 men show slightly lower correlations with each content subtest, but tend to show that each content subtest measures intelligence equally well. These correlations range from .51 (Officers' ratings and Analogies) to .63 (Officers' ratings and Synonym-Antonym).[3] Inasmuch as the content subtests have been shown to have equal validity as measures of intelligence against external criteria, the conclusion that some content subtests decline differentially with increasing age would have to be submitted to experimental verification in respect to differential relationships with increasing age against an external criterion of intelligence. Before the inference can be made that some contents penalize older subjects to a greater extent than others, empirical evidence is required to show that the validity of each content subtest as determined by an external criterion of intelligence has diminished with age as compared with the validity of the content subtest at an earlier age.

Weisenburg, Roe, and McBride [31] investigated the test results of seventy normal hospitalized adults aged 20 to 60. They concluded that differences in age did not affect test scores significantly. They, too, compared mean scores on different subtests for increasing age groups. While they point out that high points in performance in different contents apparently occur at different ages, they also show that the course of development and decline varies with age in different content performances. Scores on most language tests and arithmetic tests in-

[2] R. M. Yerkes (ed.), *Psychological Examining in the United States Army*, p. 304. Memoirs of the National Academy of Science, Vol. 15. Government Printing Office, Washington, D. C., 1921.

[3] *Ibid.*, p. 440.

cluded in their battery were well maintained in the 30's. Such facts lead to the conclusion that development in these content areas continues not only beyond adolescence, but also up to and even beyond age 30. The investigators attribute the increase in verbal and arithmetic abilities through the 30's to the fact that such abilities involve activities within the experience of older as well as younger adults. Early maturation, however, is noted on subtests involving analogies and non-language tests, followed by a subsequent rapid decline. The relatively early maturation is attributed to the early decline in motor and perceptual skills, and primarily those skills dependent upon speed rather than diligence. They suggest also the possibility of decline in spatial ability as a concomitant of drop in analogies score.

Norris [22], too, reports that the older adult appears less successful with some types of test content than with others. He, however, attributes differential decline to the quantity and recency of schooling. He demonstrates that the quality and specificity of vocational experiences of adults affects retention of some test abilities, while other abilities appear to be forgotten or lost through disuse. Comparing employed and unemployed adults in the age range of 15–60 years with school children on school achievement in various subjects measured by the Stanford Achievement test and intelligence test scores on the Otis Higher Form A, he concludes that apparently there is no large or consistent decline of general intelligence with age, within the groups tested for his study, and that gain or loss in achievement test performance is related to both length of time elapsing since the individual left school and the relationships between test content and specific vocational experiences. Norris indicates that certain school subjects deteriorate greatly with time, even when measured by examinations which are selected for their functional approach and which minimize mere memory for specific factual details. Further evidence relating to decline in intelligence test scores with age, and in specific contents with age has been reviewed by Weisenburg, Roe, and McBride [31], Brody [4], and Lorge [13], [14].

It has been suggested that certain contents may make for

differential decline insofar as speed affects score. Speed would affect to a large extent those contents related to abilities long dormant, which would require a longer adjustment or relearning process by older subjects. Lorge [18] has shown that the effect of age upon intelligence may be a function of the test used, depending on whether the test is timed or untimed. He tested 143 adults ranging in age from 20 to over 70 years of age with the I.E.R. Intelligence Scale CAVD, which is essentially a power test. In addition, he gave them five speed-power intelligence tests, including the Otis Self-Administering Test of Mental Ability and the Army Alpha. Classifying the subjects into three groups at the following age levels: I—between 20 and 25 years, II—between 27½ and 37½ years, and III—between 40 and 70 years, he equated them person for person on the basis of five forms of the CAVD. Although the three age groups showed equal intellectual power on the non-speeded CAVD test, they showed consistent decline with age on the Army Alpha, the Otis Self-Administering Test of Mental Ability, and the Thorndike Intelligence Test for High School Graduates, all of which measure speed as well as power. His results indicate that the relationship between age and ability varies with the test used to measure the ability. Thus, tests requiring adaptation to processes unfamiliar to or forgotten by older subjects would require a longer practice or "warming up" period before maximum skill in the specific ability began functioning. By applying his findings in terms of correction to the data of other investigators, Lorge found that the adjusted means did not show the same gradual decline exhibited in the obtained scores. He proposed that a correction be applied to the test scores of older adults to correct for those physiological, educational, or emotional changes that interfere with appraisal of the older person's ability to cope with mental tasks.

Sorenson [25] also shows the effect of speed on content performance. He selected 640 adults from a group of over 5,000 part-time students at the University of Minnesota to secure a uniform distribution in five-year groupings over the age range from 16 to 70. Each subject took a one-hour vocabulary test, a six-minute vocabulary test, and a forty-minute paragraph reading test. The six-minute vocabulary test was definitely regarded as a speed test, while the one-hour vocabulary and forty-minute paragraph reading tests were regarded as power tests, since the subjects were given ample time to attempt all the items. Interestingly enough, the scores in the one-hour vocabulary test rose with age, although the scores in the timed vocabulary test and the scores in the forty-minute paragraph reading test remained relatively constant. Although apparently the same abilities were being measured by the speeded and unspeeded tests, the results differed. Apparently the timed test tended to inhibit the older subjects sufficiently to depress the scores in comparison with the scores on an unspeeded test. Christian and Paterson [6] corroborate this conclusion in their investigation relating to extent of vocabulary recognition. They contend that growth in range of vocabulary recognition appears up to and even beyond age 60. On a fifteen-minute test of 120 vocabulary items taken from Thorndike's *Teacher's Word Book* given to freshmen students at the University of Minnesota and to parents and relatives of students, a slight but steady decline up to and beyond age 61 in total number of items correct was noted. The difference between mean scores made by college freshmen and mean scores made by adults grouped in ten-year age intervals was not, however, statistically significant. The increased variability for the older age groups suggested that their slightly lower mean scores might be attributed to the "slowing up" effect of age. Analysis of the number of items attempted by the various age groups revealed a marked slowing up in rate of work with advancing age, with statistically significant differences in rate of work between freshmen and adults. Most of the older subjects attempted all of the first sixty items, which permitted comparison of freshmen and adults on the basis of range of vocabulary knowledge, with the speed factor eliminated, by obtaining accuracy scores for the first sixty items. When this was done, reversal in trend was evident as shown by a definite increase in vocabulary scores of adults as compared with those of college freshmen.

Miles [21], too, has shown that tasks which are familiar in character or the result of experience tend to be less influenced by decrease in speed related to age. In tests depending essentially on comprehension, reasoning, and judgment, especially where experience may contribute to the goodness of the response, older adults appear to maintain their characteristic mature scoring level as long as they continue their mental practice and intellectual interest. Miles asserts that speed of response is dependent to no small extent on the physiological equipment available for psychological perception and response. When the speed factor is eliminated, the correlation coefficient between age and intelligence test score during the span of adult maturity drops from an average of .4 to .5 in various more or less homogeneous groups to .3 or less for a single heterogeneous population. Moreover, in power intelligence tests, different types of items show different degrees of age decrement in score. Miles found on the Otis seventy-five item intelligence test, administered without time limit to 400 adults, correlations between age and scores on groups of items classified into content subtests as follows: number relations —.26; arithmetical problems —.24; proverbs —.16; analogies —.10; logical selection —.09; vocabulary —.04; synonym-antonym +.01. The language functions appear to withstand aging best of all. It is these functions through which the factors of experience and the accumulations of culture are preserved, according to Miles. He states that performance in tasks requiring comprehension, reasoning, and judgment seems to register, in addition to native capacity, certain other psychological values such as the preserving effectiveness of practice and the actual increment of knowledge accumulated through years of persistent exercise. Scorable achievement in tasks of this type may be maintained through earlier repetitive exercise even when adaptive performance in unfamiliar tasks has shown decrement. Miles concludes that work of a skilled or familiar character is thus less diminished in effectiveness by motor and sensory decrepitude.

In addition to academic or school-type contents which make greater intellectual demands on older subjects, because of disuse, Wechsler [30] maintains that other types of content also show decrement in score with increasing age. Among the abilities showing least susceptibility to age on the Wechsler-Bellevue Test of Intelligence are: information, comprehension, vocabulary, and two performance tests—object assembly and picture completion. Tests showing marked decrement in score with increasing age are: repeating digits, arithmetical reasoning, digit symbol, picture arrangement, block design, and similarities. Greatest loss is shown on the substitution subtest, which is limited to one and a half minutes. Since the older subject is known to "slow up," his time limit is up by the time he has oriented himself to the new situation. According to Wechsler, for most intelligence test scores, the difference between ages 15 and 25 is for most practical purposes negligible, but above that age decline becomes appreciable and increasingly important. Although the age factor is adjusted in total score by percentile ranks for different age levels, obviously in spite of the adjustment speed must be penalizing the older subjects to some degree as shown by the differential decline in test score among the various subtests with increasing age.

In addition to test content and speed as factors causing decline in test score with age, changes in mental organization are suggested by Balinsky's [2] findings. He analyzed Wechsler's standardization data by means of a factor analysis to show that mental traits change and undergo a reorganization during the aging process. Using age samplings at age 9 years, 12 years, 15 years, 25 to 29 years, 35 to 44 years, and 50 to 59 years, he discovered different mental factors at the various levels. At age 9 a *g* factor and a verbal factor appear. At age 12 a verbal factor, a performance factor, and a factor called *seeing relationships in social situations* appear. At age 15 a verbal factor and a performance factor appear again. Both factors are found for ages 25 to 29, plus a memory factor and a factor termed *restriction in solution*, adopted from Thurstone's primary mental abilities. At ages 35 to 44 the verbal and performance factors are still evident, plus a memory factor. At the 50 to 59 level the *g* factor found only at the nine-year level reappears in addition to a factor involving some sort of reasoning. Balinsky points out that although the same factors do not appear always at each age level, the verbal and performance factors are most consistent. He states that mental traits change and undergo reorganization over a span of years, and therefore intelligence tests must be interpreted with consideration of the individual's age. The same test, given to a person of a certain age, may not be measuring the same abilities in him that it might be measuring when given to an individual of a different age.

In an analysis of Balinsky's data, Lorge [16] found that the first factor does not contribute the same proportion to the total variance at each age level, even though this factor may be the nearest approach to a general factor of intelligence, similar to Spearman's g. In some age groups only about one-quarter of the total variance is accounted for in the first factor, whereas in other age groups almost one-half of the total variance is accounted for in this factor. Lorge suggests that the content and form of the test make significant differences in the measurement of intelligence beyond age 20 since the type of content, such as information, arithmetic, and comprehension, is undoubtedly influenced by such factors as environment and educational background. He further asserts that power and speed are undifferentiable in the Bellevue-Wechsler test and raises the question of what it is that is being measured, inasmuch as the subject is penalized for physiological changes as he gets older as well as for any mental changes which may have taken place.

Cattell [5] hypothesizes that the nature of adult intelligence consists chiefly of two characteristics: fluid abilities and crystallized abilities. Fluid ability, increasing until adolescence and then slowly declining, has the character of a purely general ability to discriminate and perceive relations. This ability is responsible for the intercorrelations or general factor found among children's tests and among speeded or adaptation-requiring tests of adults. Crystallized ability consists of discriminatory habits long established in a particular field, originally through the operation of fluid ability, but no longer requiring insightful perception for their successful operation. Although intelligence tests at all ages require the functioning of both fluid and crystallized ability, in childhood fluid abilities predominate, while in adult life the peaks of performance are determined more by the crystallized abilities. This hypothesis assumes reorganization in the structure of intelligence in which abilities functioning at one age would not be functioning in the same manner at a later age. Cattell points out that a weakness in adult intelligence tests is the lack of success which has met all efforts to discover intelligence subtests having a validity and predictive value for adults as high as those obtained for the subtest varieties used with children.

Even though the evidence tends to show decline at different rates among content subtests, with some contents declining much more rapidly than others, the problem of the validity of various contents as measures of adult intelligence has yet to be submitted to experimental verification. If it can be shown that scores on each content do not differ significantly in validity at an age that has shown differential decline among contents, then factors other than content must be contributing to the decline in test score with age. Comparing mean content scores as an index of intellectual decline in certain abilities may not warrant the conclusion that the older adult is less able intellectually on contents having lower mean scores as compared with contents having higher mean scores. The problem resolves itself into the issue of determining whether all contents are measuring adult intellectual performance equally well. Further empirical evidence is needed concerning the relationship between contents at an age postulating decline and intelligence test scores at an age showing maximum intellectual performance.

Pertinent to the problem of the relative validity of contents as measures of intelligence at an age at which differential decline has been observed is the problem of reliability of contents over a period of time. While contents may be equally valid, if they show age differences in reliability, some may provide substantially more stable measures of adult ability than others. Since there is evidence that the abilities measured at one age may not be the identical abilities being measured at another age, as indicated by Balinsky and Cattell, only by test and retest of sample populations over a span of years could such evidence be obtained. Because of the difficulty of following up identical sample populations, relatively few longitudinal or follow-up studies of adult intelligence have been undertaken. One of the first investigations was made by Lorge [15] who retested after a period of ten years a group of men first tested when they were at or about age 14. Among the tests he gave were two which may be considered measures of intelligence: the Thorndike-McCall Reading Scale and the I.E.R. Arithmetic Test. The correlation coefficients between the initial test and the retest after ten years were as follows: reading scale .57; arithmetic test .60. These coefficients can be interpreted only in the light of their reliability coefficients. The estimated reliabilities at the first testing (based on retest with time interval negligible) were as follows: reading scale .77; arithmetic test .76. Lorge concludes that such evidence leaves little doubt that the retest coefficients are diminishing with time. He states:

In general, therefore, time diminishes the predictive value of the test for itself. This may be attributed to several causes: the initial reliability, growth, environmental factors, and time, and the limitations of the test itself. The probability is that the limitation of the test itself is the primary factor in the reduction of the retest coefficient. Tests are designed for a limited age or grade range. Whenever tests are applied outside the designed range the retest or reliability coefficient must of necessity be reduced.

From this the inference may be drawn that on a test standardized on a young population, the wider the age discrepancy between groups, the less reliable the test becomes for the older group. If differences in reliability are evident among test contents, then the less reliable contents will penalize older subjects still further. Unless the test is so standardized that norms are established for each age group to which the test is to be administered, the test will progressively penalize subjects as age increases. That tests diminish in reliability even with tests like the Stanford-Binet, which measures as unitary a trait as general intelligence, has been shown by R. L. Thorndike [28]. For repeated Binet examinations given within a single month the correlation is approximately .89, and for repeated examinations given sixty months apart the correlation is approximately .70. Inasmuch as age differences in reliability among specific contents may be a factor influencing differential decline, this aspect of the problem will also be investigated.

To recapitulate, the evidence tends to show that in adult intelligence tests not only does total test score decline with increasing age, but various test contents decline differentially, with little or no decline in contents such as vocabulary, synonym-antonym, information, practical judgment, which are retained and improved with constant use, and with marked decline in contents such as arithmetic, analogies, following directions, which involve processes suffering from disuse. It has been suggested that decline in test score may be a function of the nature of the content. Factors such as length of time elapsing since termination of schooling, physiological deterioration reflected in the "slowing up" process, mental reorganization occurring in the developmental process, and diminishing reliability of test contents have been presented as contributory to apparent decline in performance on certain contents. Because some contents as compared with other contents appear to contribute to decline in test score with increasing age, it follows that contents most susceptible to age would be less valid measures of adult intelligence. Such contents would influence test scores unfavorably for adults. The problem with which this investigation is concerned is that of the validity of different contents as measures of intelligence at an age at which differential decline has been alleged.

In most of the investigations of decline in content test score with increasing age, content status has not been viewed in its relationship to some earlier measure of intelligence. Since evidence has not been available concerning intellectual level of sample populations at crucial developmental points, the conclusions that have been reached concerning content test score decline with age have been based on the assumption that hypothetically the maximum or peak intellectual development of the various age groups was comparable. Once the assumption has been made that age groups being compared had all attained an approximately equal level of intelligence at maturity, then differences between mean scores attained on specific content might be attributed to age and its concomitants, such as experience, differences in schooling, cultural differences, and physiological deterioration. Obviously individuals do not remain intellectually static over many years, but reflect the influences of the various factors mentioned. Undoubtedly such influences will affect test score as the individual gets older.

To prove empirically that test content differentially influences the test score of the older adult, it is imperative to know his intellectual status at or near maximum test intelligence. Then contents which show lower validity at the later age than other contents against the criterion of intelligence test score at or near the maximum of test intelligence may be said to show decline. The chief obstacle in a longitudinal study of this type, however, is the difficulty of following up subjects for a sufficient length of time to secure evidence of their intellectual performance at critical periods.

The necessity of using a longitudinal approach has been recognized and emphasized by many investigators of the problem of age changes in intelligence. Wechsler [30] asserts that any mental deterioration measurement involves three separate problems: (1) the reliable measurement of the individual's actual or present functioning ability; (2) evaluation of his previous functioning level; (3) expression of the difference between the two in meaningful, quantitative terms. Miles [20] has also expressed the need of a longitudinal survey in which data must be secured from results of a series of measurements representative of whole populations at critical life periods and forming ability outlines or profiles at these critical points. In her statement that intelligence tests used on older people fail to take into consideration the original intellectual level of the individual being tested, Gilbert [8] also indicates the need for longitudinal study. She points out that even though a group of old people score at the average or below the average of a group of young people on certain tests, this fact does not indicate whether or not any individual in the group has suffered a decline in mental ability. An individual who scores above the average may actually be deteriorated, in that he does poorly as compared with what he once could do. His original level of intellect must first be known, therefore, before it is possible to determine whether or not any deterioration has taken place.

The importance of determining original intellectual level before evaluation could be made of amount of decline has also been indicated by Babcock [1], who suggests an approach to such an evaluation. On the assumption that vocabulary shows little or no intellectual deterioration, Babcock assumes vocabulary test score as indicative of original or peak intellectual level. The discrepancy between assumed basic intellectual level and scores on tests of immediate reproduction, learning requiring more concentration, motor control, and old learning indicates the subject's functioning level. The difference between the subject's score and the norm for persons of his intellectual level is termed the "efficiency index." According to Babcock's technique, it is imperative first to establish original intellectual status before amount of decline in specific abilities can be estimated.

To determine to what extent the content of adult intelligence tests at a later age is measuring the same ability known as intelligence (as reflected by an intelligence test score) at or near maximum test intelligence, a group would have to be followed up over a sufficient length of time to have been tested at both the early and the later age.

Most of the studies comparing age groups in intelligence have used the cross-sectional method because this technique lends itself to testing on an extensive scale more readily than the longitudinal method. In this study, both the longitudinal method and a modified application of the cross-sectional method will be used in analyzing the data.

Assuming that a longitudinal study could be made of an identical population, in which intellectual status as determined by an intelligence test score at or near a maximum of test intelligence was known, then the relationship between intelligence test score at or near its maximum and some later measurement of intelligence could be found. If the contents of the later intelligence test could be treated as independent measures of intelligence, then the relationship between each of the contents at the later age and intelligence test score at or near its maximum could be determined. This would be evidence of the validity of each content. It follows, then, that if the contents do not differ in validity as measures of intelligence, the correlations with the earlier measure of intelligence would show no differences among themselves.

In addition, if the correlations between each content with an external criterion of intelligence twenty years earlier and the correlations between each content at the earlier age with the external criterion also do not differ in validity, then there would be no age differences in validity. Therefore, any one content would provide as good measure of intelligence as any other content.

From the issues arising in the measurement of intellectual performance of adults, the following hypothesis has been formulated and will be tested: *Variation in the content of intelligence tests at the adult level influences estimates of intellectual ability.*

This study will seek:

1. To determine the relationships between several types of content used in adult intelligence tests and an intelligence test score at a criterion developmental point.

2. To determine the relationships between several types of content used in intelligence tests and an intelligence test score at a criterion developmental point when the measure of speed is controlled.

3. To determine the contribution of the contents to intelligence test score.

CHAPTER II

A LONGITUDINAL STUDY OF A
FOLLOW-UP GROUP

THIS IS A STUDY of the relationship between each of several types of content in an adult test of intelligence and some criterion of intelligence. If the intelligence test score of each individual at or near age 14 (a year at which test intelligence has frequently been demonstrated to be near maximum) were taken as a criterion and if performance on subtests of each of several different contents within an intelligence test were shown for the same individual at age 34 (a year at which test intelligence is not considered to be at a maximum), then the relationship between the intelligence test score at age 14 and each of the content subtests at age 34 could be estimated. The differences in the relationship between criterion or early intelligence test score and each content subtest at age 34 would be measures of the variation in content on intelligence tests. The variation in the correlation of each content subtest with the criterion of intelligence would indicate the degree to which such contents weight an intelligence test score differently for adults as contrasted with children.

With the standardized intelligence tests now in use, test intelligence appears to approach maximum between ages 13 and 20, usually closer to 13 than to 20. Terman and Merrill [26] maintain that the difference in intellectual ability between the average child of 15 and the average child of 16 is so slight that it can barely be detected by the most elaborate mental tests. Increment beyond this point, they state, has not been clearly demonstrated for unselected subjects. The precise determination of the terminal age at which unselected subjects cease to improve in mean score is made difficult by failure to secure unselected test populations above the age of 14 or 15. However, Terman and Merrill found that yearly gain begins to decrease after the age of 13 and by the age of 16 it has become approximately zero. For this reason, they entirely disregarded chronological age beyond 16 in computing the I.Q. They state: "In view of the fact that age improvement ceases gradually rather than abruptly, we begin at 13 years to disregard increasing fractions of successive chronological age increments. From 13 to 16 we cumulatively drop one out of every three additional months of chronological age and all of it after 16." According to their standardization, mental ages above 13 years cease to have the same significance as at lower levels, since they are no longer equivalent to the median performances of unselected populations of the corresponding chronological ages. Hollingworth [10] also places intelligence test performance of the average adult at approximately age 14. In describing the average adult, he states: "Upon being given intelligence tests of the standardized sort, involving literate performance, the score received would not significantly exceed that which would be made by average adolescents at their fourteenth year." Hollingworth points out that even though by the close of the adolescent period intellectual development commonly reaches its maximum, nevertheless knowledge and skill, acquired through learning as distinguished from growth, may increase until late in life. On the other hand, the average constitutions cease to grow mentally in the early years of adolescence. Pintner [24] also places the terminal point of intellectual growth as shown by test intelligence in early adolescence. Pintner has shown that when the I.Q.'s of high school children in five schools are calculated, using age 16 as the basis, the median I.Q. tends to decrease from the first to the fourth year, a result absolutely contradictory to what might be expected, since the duller students will have been eliminated before reaching the fourth year. When age 14 is used as the upper limit, the median I.Q. shows a decided increase with each year of schooling. Pintner suggests: "It would seem, therefore, best at present with our rough tests as they are now standardized to use CA 14 as a basis for the calculation of I.Q.'s for all cases above these ages." Freeman and Flory [7], using a selected population, have placed the age of maturation in test intelligence approximately between ages 15 and 20. Jones and Conrad [11] place the peak of test maturation between ages 18 and 21. Finer measures than the instruments available at the present time may well show that test intelligence may continue to grow even beyond this age. For the purposes of the present investigation, test intelligence at age 14 was accepted as indicative of maximum test intelligence for an average group.

Four requirements would have to be met for an appraisal of the relationship of content to intelligence test score: first, a sample of a population must have been tested at or near the maximum of test intelligence with an adequate test of intelligence; second, this sample must have been tested many years later with another adequate intelligence test; third, the later intelligence test must have been of sufficient length and variety in items so that the items could be classified into subtests by content; fourth, the scores on each of the separate contents must be considered as subtests of intelligence at age 34 or thereabouts.

The four requirements were satisfied by the data[1] from a sample of a population which first was tested during the years 1921–1922. At the time of the first test, the subjects were at or near 14 years of age. All in all, 826 boys, a representative sample of classes in the second term of the eighth grade in elementary schools in the Borough of Manhattan, New York, were tested.[2] Of this group of 826 boys, a sample of 131 were retested on another test of intelligence twenty years later. The 131 individuals who returned for retesting may be considered a random sample of the original 1921–1922 population.[3] The early test was the Arith-Re test, a combination formed from

[1] These data were made available to the investigator by the Institute of Educational Research, Teachers College, Columbia University.

[2] E. L. Thorndike and Others, *Prediction of Vocational Success*. The Commonwealth Fund, New York, 1934.

[3] I. Lorge and R. Blau, "Reading Comprehension of Adults," *Teachers College Record*, Vol. 43, No. 3, December, 1941, p. 192.

the I.E.R. Arithmetical Problem-Solving Test (Form B) and the Thorndike-McCall Reading Scale (Form 8).[4] The arithmetic test consists of twenty-one problems involving knowledge of fractions, percentages, and whole numbers, scored for number of problems correctly answered. The reading scale consists of nine passages, prose and verse, arranged in order of increasing difficulty. Comprehension is tested by several questions on each passage. The score is number right, which is converted to a T-score.

The composite score of the I.E.R. Arithmetical Problem-Solving Test (Form B) and the Thorndike-McCall Reading Scale (Form 8), weighted to equalize approximately the contribution of each—hereinafter referred to as the I.E.R. Arith-Re test—was considered as a test of intelligence.[5]

Toops[6] justified the use of the I.E.R. Arith-Re test as an adequate measure of intelligence in the following passage:

The value of many of the current intelligence scales is impaired by reason of their high susceptibility to improvement through practice. Ratings from such a scale will generally become higher and higher as successive forms of the test are taken by the test subject. This variation in ratings due to practice improvement does not hold in the case of arithmetic and reading, ratings from which are more nearly constant, due to the fact that at any one particular time both reading and arithmetic have been almost maximally practiced. If a weighted combination of a good arithmetic and a good reading test would correlate as highly on the average with the present intelligence scales as the average correlations of such intelligence scales with all others, then we would be justified in assuming that for practical purposes such a test is as valid an intelligence measure for the general school population as the current intelligence tests.

Toops, moreover, obtained evidence about the validity of the Arith-Re test as a measure of intelligence. He correlated it with

[4] A detailed description of these tests may be found in H. A. Toops, *Tests for Vocational Guidance of Children Thirteen to Sixteen.* Contributions to Education, No. 136, Bureau of Publications, Teachers College, Columbia University, New York, 1923.

[5] The Arith-Re score is obtained by adding three times the raw score on the arithmetic test to the T-score on the reading scale.

[6] Toops, *op. cit.,* p. 11.

the Haggerty Delta 2 Intelligence Test and with the National Intelligence Test. For 164 New York City school children in the age range 11 to 15 years, Arith-Re correlated .72 with Haggerty Delta 2 and .69 with the National Intelligence Test, and Haggerty Delta 2 correlated .76 with the National Intelligence Test. These results demonstrated that the Arith-Re test correlates about as well with other group measures of intelligence as other group intelligence tests correlate with each other. For practical purposes, therefore, the early test of intelligence, Arith-Re, may be considered a valid instrument.

The test given later was the Otis Self-Administering Test of Mental Ability (Higher Examination: Form B), under the twenty-minute directions. In the standardization process, Otis determined the validity of each item in this test by its ability to distinguish between good and poor high school students. These students had been divided into a "good" group and a "poor" group, with the same number taken from each grade for both groups. The "good" group constituted the young students, and the "poor" group the old students, but both groups had the same average educational status, although they had achieved that status at different rates. According to Otis,[7] the rate at which a student can progress through school is predicted by the mental-ability test. Therefore, he chose this criterion by which to judge the validity of each item in the test. The number of times each item was passed by each group was found and those items were chosen to be included in the test which showed a distinct number of passes by the "good" group over the number of passes by the "poor" group even though the median age of the "good" group was more than two years less fact, Otis[10] clearly indicates his position:

The Otis test consists of seventy-five items with examples of the varieties of content commonly used in paper-and-pencil group intelligence tests. That these items are classifiable into readily recognizable content categories has been shown by Miles

---

[7] A. S. Otis, *Otis Self-Administering Tests of Mental Ability. Manual of Directions and Key (Revised)*. World Book Company, Yonkers-on-Hudson, N. Y., 1928.

and Bingham. In a study of the relationship of intelligence to age, Miles [21] classified the items of the Otis test into seven content categories:[8] number relations, arithmetical problems, proverbs, analogies, logical selection, vocabulary, synonym-antonym. Bingham [3], in describing the Otis test, considered the items classifiable into content categories of information, arithmetic, number series completion, recognition of opposites, analogies, understanding of proverbs, logical inferences, and practical judgment. Moreover, Otis[9] as author, suggests:

To be sure, the items fall quite obviously into certain rough classifications; there are some on finding the opposite of a word, some on completing analogies, some on detecting similarities, some on arranging disarranged sentences, some on simple arithmetic, and so on, but these are all fairly obvious.

Miles, Bingham, and Otis apparently are agreed that the Otis items are classifiable into content categories. Furthermore, there is agreement as to some of the categories; all three mention categories involving vocabulary, analogies, and proverbs content. The classification of items into content categories is to some extent arbitrary. Otis chose the items primarily for their ability to discriminate between good and poor students, not because they belonged in convenient content categories. As a matter of fact, Otis[10] clearly indicates his position:

I think of each item as measuring quite a number of aspects of mental ability, each one measuring all, or nearly all, of these aspects but merely in differing degrees. For example, every item measures to some extent the ability to read, which we may subdivide into the ability to perceive the printed word, to associate the meaning of the word with its perception, the ability to combine the meanings of the separate words of a sentence into a synthesized meaning. It also measures the ability to direct one's thinking in accordance with the directions inherent in this meaning, the ability to execute the

---

[8] Miles states in a personal communication regarding these classifications that his item groupings were to some extent abitrary, but for the most part they were classified according to the obvious item content.

[9] In a personal communication to the investigator.

[10] *Ibid.*

directions as understood, as for example, to choose a right answer, note its number, put the number in the proper parenthesis, etc. . . .

Using the classifications suggested by Miles, by Bingham, and by Otis, the author chose eight content classifications of the Otis items: synonym-antonym, arithmetic, information, analogies, vocabulary, logical selection, proverbs, and directions. To determine the extent of agreement among competent judges in assigning each item to a specific classification, five graduate students in psychology were asked to classify each item of the Otis test into the eight categories. In the directions to the judges, the intent was to minimize attention to the form of the item so that the content would be dominant in their classification. The judges were told that all items involving the use of numbers were to be classified as arithmetic; items involving word knowledge were to be classified as vocabulary; items involving specialized type of information were to be classified as information; items involving the following of directions were to be classified as directions; items involving inference were to be classified as logical selection; and items involving likenesses or opposites of words were to be classified as synonym-antonym.

The five judges agreed completely on the classification of sixty-five of the seventy-five items. On another four items, four of the five judges agreed as to their classification, and on the remaining six items, three of the judges agreed as to their classification. Table I shows the classification of the items and the percent of agreement for each item.

The items within each of the eight content categories were considered as constituting a subtest. The averages for each of these eight content subtests and the averages for the number of items attempted in each content subtest, together with their standard deviations, are given in Table II. The ratio of the averages for the subtests to the averages for the attempts is also given in order to show the relative difficulty of each of the subtests. The means for the Arith-Re test at age 14 and the total Otis test at age 34 are also given. The time limit of twenty minutes operated to prevent many of the subjects from attempting

TABLE I

Content Subtest Classification by Five Judges of Items of Otis Test of Mental Ability (Higher Examination: Form B)

Content Subtest	Number of Items in Each Subtest	Complete Agreement Among Five Judges for Items Number:	Less than Complete Agreement Among Five Judges for Items Number:
Synonym-Antonym	9	1, 6, 10, 17, 25, 29, 38, 42	56—Syn.-Ant., 3 judges; Log. Sel., 2 judges: 60% agreement
Arithmetic	13	2, 9, 18, 20, 31, 39, 44, 49, 58, 62, 65, 68, 71	
Information	7	3, 7, 14, 21, 23	40—Inf., 3 judges; Log. Sel., 2 judges: 60% agreement 47—Inf., 3 judges; Log. Sel., 2 judges: 60% agreement
Analogies	7	8, 15, 27, 41, 25, 56, 63	
Vocabulary	9	19, 28, 37, 46, 52, 61	51—Vocab., 3 judges; Log. Sel., 1 judge; Inf., 1 judge: 60% agreement 54—Vocab., 3 judges; Log. Sel., 1 judge; Inf., 1 judge: 60% agreement 60—Vocab., 4 judges; Inf., 1 judge: 80% agreement
Logical Selection	11	5, 22, 24, 35, 36, 43, 50, 67, 70	16—Log. Sel., 3 judges; Inf., 2 judges: 60% agreement 26—Log. Sel., 4 judges; Inf., 1 judge: 80% agreement
Proverbs	6	11, 12, 13, 32, 33, 34	
Directions	13	4, 30, 48, 52, 57, 64, 66, 69, 72, 73, 74	59—Dir., 4 judges; Arith., 1 judge: 80% agreement 75—Dir., 4 judges; Log. Sel., 1 judge: 80% agreement

23

each item of the test. The average number of items attempted on the Otis test was 47.6. Eleven of the thirteen items in the Directions subtest are placed after item 47; five of the nine Vocabulary items are placed after item 47. The differences in

TABLE II

INTERCORRELATIONS AMONG CONTENT SUBTESTS, ARITH-RE, OTIS SCORE, AND "ITEMS ATTEMPTED," TOGETHER WITH MEANS AND STANDARD DEVIATIONS OF EACH OF THE SPECIFIED VARIABLES: FOLLOW-UP GROUP $(N = 131)$

Variables	1	2	3	4	5	6	7	8	9	10	11
1. Synonym-Ant.	..	.51	.60	.56	.55	.63	.50	.45	.52	.74	..
2. Arithmetic		..	.66	.58	.64	.73	.48	.70	.55	.84	..
3. Information			..	.59	.58	.66	.55	.50	.54	.79	..
4. Analogies				..	.65	.68	.54	.64	.44	.81	..
5. Vocabulary					..	.67	.44	.70	.48	.82	..
6. Logical Sel.						..	.54	.65	.51	.88	..
7. Proverbs							..	.37	.51	.68	..
8. Directions								..	.44	.74	..
9. Arith-Re									..	.62	.33
10. Otis										..	.74
11. Attempts											..
Mean	5.81	5.37	5.08	2.29	3.20	5.08	3.92	1.64	82.1	32.4	47.6
S.D.	1.84	2.30	1.52	1.67	2.30	2.30	1.75	1.90	12.9	12.5	12.0
Mean Attempted	7.70	7.28	6.25	4.69	4.68	7.71	5.73	3.50			
S.D.	1.27	2.11	.95	1.38	2.47	1.85	.82	2.43			
Ratio of Mean Passed to Mean Attempted	.75	.74	.81	.48	.68	.66	.68	.46			

content subtest performance, however, may be a matter not only of item opportunity, but also of item difficulty. The items of the test are arranged in order of difficulty;[11] therefore, those subtests containing a relatively large proportion of items toward the end of the test would be expected to be more difficult than subtests containing a majority of items toward the first half of the test. When the average number of items passed in each subtest is compared with the average number of items attempted in each subtest, the ratios from high to low are as

[11] A. S. Otis, *Otis Self-Administering Tests of Mental Ability. Manual of Directions and Key (Revised)*, p. 3. World Book Company, Yonkers-on-Hudson, N. Y., 1928.

follows: information, synonym-antonym, arithmetic, proverbs, vocabulary, logical selection, analogies, and directions.

The performance of the sample on total Otis is at the norm for adults.[12]

Each of the eight content subtests on the Otis test was considered as a separate measure of intelligence. Since the criterion of test intelligence was the Arith-Re test score at age 14, the correlation between it and each Otis content subtest score at age 34 would be considered evidence of the validity of each content as a measure of intelligence. If there are no significant differences among the correlations between each of the eight Otis content subtest scores at age 34 with Arith-Re score, then it may be concluded that each content subtest is an equally valid measure of test intelligence at age 34. If, however, significant differences are present among the relationships between the content subtest and Arith-Re score, it may be concluded that some content subtests are less valid measures of intelligence at age 34 than others.

Table II presents the product-moment correlations between each of the content subtests and Arith-Re. The correlation between the total Otis and the Arith-Re criterion is $+.62$; the correlation between each subtest and the criterion ranges from $+.44$ to $+.55$. On retests of the Binet test after five years, Thorndike [28] found the retest coefficient to be approximately .70. Applying his formula for determining retest coefficient, the retest on the Binet after twenty years would be substantially lower than the coefficients between Arith-Re and total Otis score, and Arith-Re and each of the content subtests. In other words, there is a higher correlation between Arith-Re and the Otis test after an interval of twenty years than the estimated retest coefficient on the Binet test after twenty years. Moreover, each of the content subtests shows a higher relationship with Arith-Re than would be expected to be found on the Binet retest after such a long interval.

The slight reduction in relationship between Arith-Re and

12 *Ibid.*, p. 6.

the content subtests as compared with Arith-Re and total Otis score is undoubtedly influenced by the unreliability introduced by the smaller number of items in the content subtests. Five out of eight of the content subtests correlate above +.50 with Arith-Re. Thus intelligence as measured by Arith-Re at age 14 is measured to a large extent by all of the Otis contents at age 34. Inasmuch as there are no statistically significant differences among the coefficients,[13] all the content subtests may be considered not to differ in validity as measures of intelligence at age 34.

Since there were no significant differences among the relationships between each content subtest at age 34 and the external criterion (Arith-Re at age 14), the relationships present among the content subtests themselves were estimated as another indicator of their relative validity as measures of adult intelligence. The intercorrelations among the content subtests also are given in Table II. These range from +.73 (Arithmetic and Logical Selection) to +.37 (Proverbs and Directions). Twenty-four of the twenty-eight intercorrelations are +.50 or higher. The intercorrelations show that each of the content subtests is a good measure of intelligence at age 34. As might be expected, each of the content subtests correlates highly with total Otis score. There is a range in coefficients from +.88 to +.68.

It has been demonstrated thus far that the subtests do not differ in validity among themselves. The hypothesis that particular contents of adult intelligence tests affect estimates of adult intellectual ability or tend to exhibit differential declines does not hold for the Otis test when content subtest scores at age 34 are correlated against a known intelligence test score obtained at age 14. It must be pointed out that demonstration of the null hypothesis does not prove that the subtests are equal. The null hypothesis may have been maintained because of the unreliability of the subtests.

Factors such as reliability of the content subtests, correction

---

[13] All coefficients were first changed to their Fisher *z* equivalents before testing for significance.

for attenuation of the validity coefficients, and the influence of a measure of speed on the validity coefficients must be investigated to determine the effect of any of these factors upon the relative validity of content subtests as measures of intelligence at age 34.

The problem of reliability is dealt with first since it is essential to know whether certain item contents are more reliable than others as adult intelligence measures. Given two measures of approximately equal validity, the more reliable measure is the more useful and should be retained as a more desirable measuring instrument. Content reliability is dependent in this investigation upon both content classification and item placement within the test. Reliability coefficients obtained by use of the Kuder-Richardson Formula No. 20[14] are given in Table III. There is a range from $+.80$ (Vocabulary) to $+.56$ (Information). That content subtests are influenced by item placement, a combination in this case of both item opportunity and item difficulty, as well as by inequalities in the number of items per category, is evident. There are no significant differences among twenty-four pairs of coefficients. Four pairs of coefficients show significant differences at the 1 per cent level. All four include coefficients of two categories, Vocabulary and Directions, as one of the pairs. It has been stated earlier that these two content subtests had a majority of their items in the latter part of the test, which was not reached by most of the group. Both differ from Information and Synonym-Antonym reliability coefficients, the latter two being the easiest subtests in point of difficulty. It can be stated, therefore, that not one of the eight content subtests of the Otis test is consistently more reliable than any other. Each content can be used as a measure of adult intelligence with approximately equal reliability.

The original validity coefficients were also corrected for attenuation to see whether errors in measurement of the various contents might possibly have obscured the true relationships between the various contents and Arith-Re. The corrected

[14] G. F. Kuder and M. W. Richardson, "The Theory of the Estimation of Test Reliability," *Psychometrika*, Vol. 2, No. 3, September, 1937, pp. 151–160.

coefficients are presented in Table III. There is a range from +.79 (Arith-Re and Information) to +.55 (Arith-Re and Directions). The corrected correlation coefficient between Arith-Re score and Information score is spuriously higher than any of the other corresponding relationships since it is a function of the greater unreliability of the Information content. Twenty-four pairs of the corrected relationships show no significant differences between them. Four pairs of relationships show

TABLE III

CORRELATION OF EACH CONTENT SUBTEST WITH THE CRITERION (ARITH-RE) CORRECTED FOR ATTENUATION, AND INDEPENDENT OF THE NUMBER OF "ATTEMPTS," TOGETHER WITH THE ESTIMATED RELIABILITY COEFFICIENT FOR EACH CONTENT SUBTEST: FOLLOW-UP GROUP ($N = 131$)

Content Subtests	Correlation with Arith-Re Corrected for Attenuation	Net r with Arith-Re "Attempts" Partialed Out	Reliability Coefficient (Kuder-Richardson Formula No. 20)
1. Synonym-Antonym	.74	.46	.58
2. Arithmetic	.70	.50	.71
3. Information	.79	.48	.56
4. Analogies	.60	.37	.63
5. Vocabulary	.58	.42	.80
6. Logical Selection	.66	.45	.70
7. Proverbs	.66	.48	.69
8. Directions	.55	.40	.75

significant differences at the 1 per cent level. Three of these pairs involve Arith-Re and Information as one of the pairs. The fourth pair showing significant difference is Arith-Re and Synonym-Antonym with Arith-Re and Directions. To a degree, then, the unreliability of the subtests may contribute to the inference that the tests do not differ among themselves in validity. Aside from this, it may be stated that the data, freed of errors of measurement, exhibit no significant differences among the relationships. In general, the conclusion that the eight Otis content subtests do not differ in validity as measures of intelligence at age 34, when another intelligence test score at age 14 is used as the criterion, is reaffirmed. Thus the hypothesis that content of adult intelligence tests influences adult intelligence test scores differentially would appear untenable, particularly with respect to the Otis test.

One of the controversial issues concerning differential decline in contents with increasing age has been that of the effect of speed. Therefore, an effort was made to control the effect of speed to some degree. In this study, the measure of speed is designated by the average number of items *attempted* in each content subtest. "Attempts" as a measure of speed has been used previously in investigations of intelligence test performance as related to age by both Yerkes [32] and Jones and Conrad [11].

In this investigation the control of the number of "attempts" in each content subtest was particularly important since the twenty-minute time limit and the relative item placement were such as to limit the relative opportunity for each content subtest to contribute maximally to the measure of adult intelligence at age 34. Eliminating the influence of speed (as measured by "attempts") would thus indirectly equalize item opportunity in the content subtests. The net correlation between Arith-Re score and content subtest score with "attempts" partialed out are listed in Table III. Naturally, there is a slight reduction in relationship between each content score and Arith-Re. The range is from +.50 (Arith-Re and Arithmetic) to +.37 (Arith-Re and Analogies). There are no significant differences among the net relationships.

Thus, this investigation tends to prove that speed (as measured by "attempts") has little, if any, influence on the relative validity of the eight content subtests as measures of intelligence at age 34. The importance of this finding is emphasized by the fact that, in this study, the control of "attempts" has tended to equate indirectly operation of both item placement and item difficulty in the evaluation of the relative effectiveness of the eight content subtests. All the statistical refinements have succeeded in reinforcing the first finding: namely, that each of the eight content subtests of the Otis test does not differ in validity and reliability as a measure of intelligence at age 34, judged by the criterion of intelligence test score at age 14 (Arith-Re). Inasmuch as the content subtests do not differ in validity as measures of intelligence at age 34 based on relationship of these content scores and criterion intelligence test score at age 14, the hypothesis that the content of an adult intelligence test influences intelligence test score does not appear to be tenable. Moreover, when account is taken of the reliability of the content subtests, the correction for unreliability of the measures, and the elimination of the effect of speed to some degree, the hypothesis is still nullified.

CHAPTER III

A CROSS-SECTIONAL STUDY OF A
STATIC GROUP

THE PREVIOUS CHAPTER showed that for a follow-up group tested
at age 14 with an intelligence test (Arith-Re) and retested at
age 34 with another intelligence test (Otis Self-Administering
Test of Mental Ability—Higher Examination: Form B), in
which the items were classified into independent content
subtests, there were no significant differencés in the relationships between each content subtest at age 34 and criterion intelligence test score at age 14. Had the performance of the
same group been known on content subtests at age 14, the
relationships between each of the content subtests at age 14
and criterion intelligence test score at age 14 could have been
estimated. The relationships between each content subtest at
age 14 and Arith-Re at age 14 would indicate the relative
validities of the content subtests as measures of intelligence at
age 14. Then these validity coefficients of content subtest at
age 14 and Arith-Re at age 14 could be compared with the
validity coefficients of content subtests at age 34 and Arith-Re
at age 14. Variation in the relationship between (1) each of the
content subtests at age 34 and intelligence test score at age 14,
and (2) each of the content subtests at age 14 and intelligence
test score at age 14 would indicate those contents which may
weight an intelligence test score differently for adults as contrasted with children. If the content subtests at age 34 and at
age 14 do not differ in validity as measures of intelligence
against the criterion of intelligence test score at age 14—the
age at which test intelligence has been shown to be at or near
its maximum, then the conclusion would follow that factors

other than the content of the test influence differential decline among test contents.

The follow-up group had been given the Arith-Re test at age 14 and had not been given the Otis test until twenty years later. Hence it was necessary to secure a group at or near age 14, equivalent in intelligence to the follow-up group at or near age 14. This group, called the *static* group, equivalent to the follow-up group in intelligence as indicated by the Arith-Re score at age 14, could then be given the Otis test at age 14 also. From the Otis test, the content subtest scores for the static group at age 14 could be found. The relationships between content subtest score at age 14 for the static group and Arith-Re at age 14 for the static group could then be determined.

The static group was matched with the follow-up group on the basis of the following variables: age, sex, amount of schooling, total Arith-Re score, and scores on the arithmetic and reading test which make up the Arith-Re test. To obtain 131 cases in the static group matched case for case with 131 cases in the follow-up group, 296 boys were tested. They were in the eighth B grade (third month) in two metropolitan schools which the boys in the follow-up group had attended in 1921–1922.

They were given the Otis Self-Administering Test of Mental Ability (Higher Examination: Form B), with a twenty-minute time limit; the I.E.R. Arithmetical Problem-Solving Test (Form B); and the Thorndike-McCall Reading Scale (Form 8). Since the variables of amount of schooling and sex were equivalent for the follow-up and the static groups, the matching of each case in the static group to a case in the follow-up group was completed on the basis of the other four variables: T-score on the Thorndike-McCall Reading Scale, score on the I.E.R. Arithmetical Problem-Solving Test, total Arith-Re score, and age. As each case was selected from the static group to match one in the follow-up group, the scores on each of these four variables were cumulated for both groups so as to ensure approximate equivalence in score for each of these four variables. This method of matching produced equivalent mean scores and equivalent variability on Arith-Re for the static and follow-up groups. Thus, for the purposes of this investigation, the two groups may be assumed to be equivalent in criterion intelligence test score at age 14, as indicated by their Arith-Re scores.

As in the case of the follow-up group, each of the eight content subtests was treated as an independent intelligence test. The averages for each of these subtests and the averages for the number of items attempted in each content subtest, together with their standard deviations, are given in Table IV. The ratio of the averages for the subtests to the averages for the attempts is also given. The means for Arith-Re at age 14 and total Otis at age 14 are included. The group is performing slightly below the norm on the Otis.[1] The average number of items attempted on the Otis test was 44.8, and, as in the case of the follow-up group, many of the subjects in the static group never reached a large proportion of the items in the Arithmetic, Directions, and Vocabulary subtests. For the static group, when the average number of items passed in each content subtest is compared with the average number of items attempted, the content subtest order of difficulty is as follows: Information, Logical Selection, Synonym-Antonym, Vocabulary, Arithmetic, Proverbs, Directions, and Analogies. As previously discussed in Chapter II, page 27, the observed discrepancies in content performance are functions both of item placement and of item difficulty.

The correlation between Arith-Re test score at age 14 and each Otis content subtest score at age 14 would be considered evidence of the validity of each content as a measure of intelligence at age 14. No significant differences in the validity of each content subtest at age 14 against the criterion of Arith-Re score at age 14 would warrant the conclusion that the content subtests are equally valid for the measurement of intelligence at age 14. Should significantly different relationships be ob-

<hr>

[1] A. S. Otis, *Otis Self-Administering Tests of Mental Ability. Manual of Directions and Key (Revised).* World Book Company, Yonkers-on-Hudson, N. Y., 1928.

tained, however, then it could be inferred that specific contents influence intelligence test score at age 14.

Table IV also presents the product-moment correlations between each of the content subtests and Arith-Re at age 14. The intercorrelations of Arith-Re, total Otis score, and items attempted on the Otis test are also given. The correlation of +.71 between total Otis score and Arith-Re criterion indicates that both tests are measuring many of the same abilities at age 14. The coefficients between each subtest at age 14 and Arith-Re at age 14 range from +.56 to +.33. There are no statistically significant differences among any of the pairs of relationships.

TABLE IV

INTERCORRELATIONS AMONG CONTENT SUBTESTS, ARITH-RE, OTIS SCORE, AND "ITEMS ATTEMPTED," TOGETHER WITH MEANS AND STANDARD DEVIATIONS OF EACH OF THE SPECIFIED VARIABLES: STATIC GROUP ($N = 131$)

Variables	1	2	3	4	5	6	7	8	9	10	11
1. Synonym-Antonym	..	.30	.38	.43	.35	.51	.50	.45	.52	.73	..
2. Arithmetic		..	.46	.22	.30	.43	.37	.36	.56	.67	..
3. Information			..	.37	.37	.52	.36	.37	.49	.70	..
4. Analogies				..	.38	.34	.39	.35	.33	.60	..
5. Vocabulary					..	.31	.24	.38	.35	.59	..
6. Logical Selection						..	.50	.44	.50	.77	..
7. Proverbs							..	.44	.56	.71	..
8. Directions								..	.50	.66	..
9. Arith-Re									..	.71	.17
10. Otis										..	.46
11. Attempts											..
Mean	3.68	2.72	4.21	1.18	1.68	3.77	2.02	.82	81.9	20.1	44.8
S.D.	1.70	1.83	1.38	1.03	1.31	1.66	1.64	.92	12.9	7.9	10.4
Mean Attempted	7.48	6.74	6.11	4.31	4.14	7.53	5.61	2.87			
S.D.	1.18	1.81	.88	1.27	2.29	1.52	.99	1.59			
Ratio of Mean Passed to Mean Attempted	.49	.40	.70	.27	.41	.50	.36	.29			

The intercorrelations among the content subtests at age 14 (Table IV) range from +.52 (Information and Logical Selection) to +.22 (Arithmetic and Analogies). Each one of the content subtests correlates highly with the total Otis score.

There is a range in coefficient from +.77 to +.59. The intercorrelations indicate that the content subtests are approximately equally good as measures of intelligence at age 14.

Inasmuch as there are no significant differences among the content subtests at age 14 as measures of intelligence against the criterion of Arith-Re at age 14, the data were analyzed further to determine the influence of the factors of reliability, correction for attenuation, and the influence of the number of items attempted (as a measure of speed) at age 14.

Since it is important to know how reliable each of the content subtests is at age 14, reliability is considered first. In this study reliability is dependent upon both content classification and item placement within the test.

The reliability coefficients obtained by use of the Kuder-Richardson Formula No. 20,[2] are given in Table V. There is a range from +.63 (Proverbs) to +.20 (Analogies). When the reliability coefficients of each content subtest at age 14 are compared, there are no significant differences among twenty of the pairs. Eight pairs of reliability coefficients are significantly different from each other at the 1 per cent level of significance. Arithmetic shows significantly higher reliability than Information, Analogies, and Directions. Proverbs shows significantly higher reliability than Information, Analogies, Directions, and Logical Selection. Synonym-Antonym shows significantly higher reliability than Analogies. At age 14, some contents are more reliable measures of intelligence than others. According to these data, the three most reliable contents at age 14 are Proverbs, Arithmetic, and Synonym-Antonym. Since the Otis test was standardized on a high school population, the Analogies, Information, and Directions content may be too difficult for fourteen-year-olds or the time too short for this age group to attempt the items. Inasmuch as the reliability coefficients of the content subtests at age 14 showed differences in reliability, the original validity coefficients were corrected for attenuation. The corrected coefficients are also presented in Table V. The

---

[2] Kuder and Richardson, *loc. cit.*

range is from +.95 (Arith-Re and Information) to +.57 (Arith-Re and Vocabulary).

When the correlations are corrected for attenuation, the interrelationships between Arith-Re and Information, Arith-Re and Vocabulary, and Arith-Re and Logical Selection seem to

TABLE V

CORRELATION OF EACH CONTENT SUBTEST WITH THE CRITERION (ARITH-RE) CORRECTED FOR ATTENUATION, AND INDEPENDENT OF THE NUMBER OF "ATTEMPTS," TOGETHER WITH THE ESTIMATED RELIABILITY COEFFICIENT FOR EACH CONTENT SUBTEST: STATIC GROUP ($N = 131$)

Content Subtests	Correlation with Arith-Re Corrected for Attenuation	Net r with Arith-Re "Attempts" Partialed Out	Reliability Coefficient (Kuder-Richardson Formula No. 20)
1. Synonym-Antonym	.82	.51	.49
2. Arithmetic	.79	.55	.59
3. Information	.95	.48	.32
4. Analogies	.79	.31	.20
5. Vocabulary	.57	.33	.44
6. Logical Selection	.88	.48	.38
7. Proverbs	.77	.55	.63
8. Directions	.92	.49	.34

differ in validity from the other five interrelationships. This difference in some ways is very much like that discovered by Jones and Conrad [11] when they show on the Army Alpha test that after age 20 there is practically no loss in score on the Vocabulary and Information as contrasted with other subtests. This may be due to the effect of speed. To determine whether the effect of speed as measured by the number of attempts on each subtest affects the validity coefficients of any of the content subtests at age 14 against the criterion of Arith-Re at age 14, the number of items attempted in each content subtest were partialed out of the relationships. Eliminating the influence of speed would to some degree also aid in equalizing item opportunity and item difficulty. The partial correlations between each of the content subtests at age 14 and Arith-Re at age 14 (with number of items attempted in each subtest partialed out) are listed in Table V. These partial correlations range from +.55 (Arith-Re and Arithmetic; Arith-Re and Proverbs) to a +.31 (Arith-Re and Analogies). As is to be expected, there is a slight reduction in relationship (.01 to .02) between Arith-Re at age 14 and each of the content subtests at age 14. There are no significant differences among the net correlations.

Thus the results show that speed, as measured by items attempted, has little if any influence on the validity of each of the eight content subtests as measures of intelligence at age 14.

For a static group who were given both the Otis test and the Arith-Re test at age 14, each of the eight content subtests on the Otis test shows no significant differences in validity at age 14 against the criterion of intelligence test score (Arith-Re) at age 14. The content subtests show no differences in validity even when account is taken of the effect of speed (as measured by items attempted). The content reliabilities at age 14, however, show some significant differences among themselves. The Arithmetic and Proverbs contents tend to be most reliable for appraising intelligence of fourteen-year-olds. The Information, Analogies, Directions, and Logical Selection contents appear to be least reliable.

CHAPTER IV

COMPARISON OF THE FOLLOW-UP AND STATIC GROUPS

ANALYSIS OF THE DATA for the follow-up group has shown that content subtests at age 34 do not differ in validity as measures of intelligence against the criterion of intelligence test score at age 14. In addition, analysis of the data for the static group has shown that the same content subtests at age 14 do not differ in validity as measures of intelligence against the same criterion of intelligence test score at age 14. If the relationships of content subtests at age 34 and Arith-Re at age 14 (follow-up group) compared with the relationships of content subtests at age 14 and Arith-Re at age 14 (static group) show no significant differences, then it may be concluded that these contents are equally valid measures of intelligence at both ages 34 and 14. From this, the conclusion would follow that no one of these contents weights an intelligence test score in favor of individuals in either age group. If the contents show no significant differences in validity either at age 34 or at age 14, then the contention that older age groups do poorly as compared with younger age groups on some contents, such as arithmetic and analogies, cannot be attributed to the contents *per se*, but may be the result of other factors, such as amount of schooling, length of time elapsed since termination of schooling, and experience. This finding would be particularly significant for test construction purposes, for contents showing approximately equal validity and reliability over a wide age range could be used in tests for the purpose of comparing intelligence test scores of different age groups.

In order to compare the follow-up and static groups, the means and standard deviations of both groups on the Arith-Re,

Otis score, "Items Attempted," and each of the content subtests, are repeated in Table VI. As the follow-up and static groups were equated on the basis of their Arith-Re test scores at or near age 14, for both groups the mean Arith-Re score is 82, and the standard deviation is 12.9. On total Otis test score, however,

TABLE VI

MEANS AND STANDARD DEVIATIONS ON ARITH-RE, OTIS, "ITEMS ATTEMPTED,"
AND EACH OF THE CONTENT SUBTESTS: FOLLOW-UP AND STATIC GROUPS

Variables	Follow-up at Age 34 (N = 131) $\overline{\text{X}}$	s.d.	Static at Age 14 (N = 131) $\overline{\text{X}}$	s.d.
1. Synonym-Antonym	5.81	1.84	3.68	1.70
2. Arithmetic	5.37	2.30	2.72	1.83
3. Information	5.08	1.52	4.21	1.38
4. Analogies	2.29	1.67	1.18	1.03
5. Vocabulary	3.20	2.30	1.68	1.31
6. Logical Selection	5.08	2.30	3.77	1.66
7. Proverbs	3.92	1.75	2.02	1.64
8. Directions	1.64	1.90	.82	.92
9. Arith-Re	82.1	12.9	81.9	12.9
10. Otis	32.4	12.5	20.1	7.9
11. Attempts	47.6	12.0	44.8	10.4

with the difference of a twenty-year age interval in the administration of the test, the mean score for the follow-up group at age 34 is 32.4, while the mean score for the static group at age 14 is 20.1. The standard deviation is 12.5 for the follow-up group, while it is 7.9 for the static group. Even though the two groups have equivalent intelligence test scores on Arith-Re at age 14, the follow-up group at age 34 would naturally obtain proportionately higher scores on the Otis test as the result of added schooling and experience than the static group would obtain on the Otis test at age 14.

When the means of the "attempts" on the Otis test, which is used as the measure of speed, are compared for the two groups, it is obvious that the static group at age 14 is working nearly as rapidly as the follow-up group at age 34. The mean of the "attempts" for the follow-up group is 47.6 and for the static group 44.8. Even though both groups attempt almost the same number of items, the follow-up group at age 34 gets many more of the items correct than the static group at age 14, as shown by the difference in mean score. The follow-up group gets an average of 12.3 more items correct than the static group, although they are attempting approximately only three more items than the static group. The older group may be exercising greater caution in attempting only those items that they are sure they can answer correctly, while the younger group with less restraint may be attempting every item, regardless of the possibility of responding incorrectly.

The correlation coefficients between (1) each content subtest at age 34 and Arith-Re at age 14 for the follow-up group and (2) each content subtest at age 14 and Arith-Re at age 14 for the static group are repeated in Table VII. The correlation coefficients show no significant differences between any of the eight pairs of relationships. It has been demonstrated that each of the content subtests does not differ in validity at age 34 and at age 14 as measures of intelligence, judged by the criterion intelligence test score at age 14 (Arith-Re). Thus a group at age 34 and a group at age 14 appear to be measured with equal effectiveness by these content subtests. Any one of these contents in any intelligence test, taken at either age 34 or age 14, would appraise the intelligence of the subject equally well. It may be inferred, therefore, that any one of these contents, or all of them combined, or any combination of them would provide equally valid measures of intelligence at either age 34 or age 14.

Even though the contents do not differ in validity as measures of intelligence at age 34 and at age 14, if the contents differ in reliability at both ages, the contents would not be equally good as intelligence test measures at both ages and therefore might influence intelligence test score. Therefore, the reliability coefficients of each of the content subtests were compared for the follow-up and static groups. These reliability coefficients are also given in Table VII. There are no significant differences between the reliability coefficients at ages 34 and 14 of the following four content subtests: Synonym-Antonym, Arithmetic, Information, and Proverbs. Thus, these four con-

TABLE VII

CORRELATION OF EACH CONTENT SUBTEST WITH THE CRITERION (ARITH-RE), CORRECTED FOR ATTENUATION, AND INDEPENDENT OF "ATTEMPTS," TOGETHER WITH THE ESTIMATED RELIABILITY COEFFICIENTS FOR EACH CONTENT SUBTEST FOR THE FOLLOW-UP AND STATIC GROUPS (N=131)

Content Subtests	Correlation with Arith-Re at Age 14		Correlation with Arith-Re Corrected for Attenuation		Net r with Arith-Re ("Attempts" Partialed Out)		Reliability Coefficients (Kuder-Richardson Formula No. 20)	
	Follow-up at Age 34	Static at Age 14	Follow-up at Age 34	Static at Age 14	Follow-up at Age 34	Static at Age 14	Follow-up at Age 34	Static at Age 14
1. Synonym-Antonym	.52	.52	.74	.82	.46	.51	.58	.49
2. Arithmetic	.55	.56	.70	.79	.50	.55	.71	.59
3. Information	.54	.49	.79	.95	.48	.48	.56	.32
4. Analogies	.44	.33	.60	.79	.37	.31	.63	.20
5. Vocabulary	.48	.35	.58	.57	.42	.33	.80	.44
6. Logical Selection	.51	.50	.66	.88	.45	.48	.70	.38
7. Proverbs	.51	.56	.66	.77	.48	.55	.69	.63
8. Directions	.44	.50	.55	.92	.40	.49	.75	.34

tent subtests may be said not to differ in validity and reliability as measures of intelligence at ages 34 and 14. There are significant differences at ages 34 and 14 between the reliability coefficients of the following four content subtests: Analogies, Vocabulary, Logical Selection, and Directions. These four content subtests are less reliable as measures of intelligence at age 14 than they are at age 34.

Because there were significant differences between the reliability coefficients of some of the content subtests at age 34 and the reliability coefficients of these content subtests at age 14, the validity coefficients of both the follow-up and the static group corrected for attenuation were also compared. These corrected coefficients are also given in Table VII. The follow-up and static groups show no significant differences between their corrected validity coefficients for: Arith-Re and Synonym-Antonym; Arith-Re and Arithmetic; Arith-Re and Vocabulary; Arith-Re and Proverbs. The two groups do show significant differences between the corrected validity coefficients for: Arith-Re and Information; Arith-Re and Analogies; Arith-Re and Logical Selection; Arith-Re and Directions. It should be noted that three of these pairs of corrected coefficients showing statistically significant differences between the two groups include in the relationships with Arith-Re the content subtests which also show significant differences between the reliability coefficients of these content subtests. These relationships include the following content subtests: Analogies, Logical Selection, and Directions.

The net correlations between Arith-Re at age 14 and each of the content subtests at age 34 and at age 14, with "attempts" partialed out for the purpose of controlling the effect of speed, are also given in Table VII. There are no significant differences between the net correlation coefficients of the follow-up group and the static group. Even with "attempts" partialed out, each of the content subtests shows no difference in validity as a measure of intelligence at age 34 and at age 14.

For the purpose of determining which content subtests at ages 34 and 14 are contributing most to the prediction of Arith-

Re at age 14, the Beta weights of the regression equations were computed. The coefficient of multiple correlation predicting Arith-Re at age 14 from the best possible combination of the eight content subtests at age 34 is $+.66$. The coefficient of multiple correlation predicting Arith-Re at age 14 from the eight content subtests at age 14 is $+.75$. The Beta weights of the regression equations for both the follow-up group and the static group are listed in Table VIII. Synonym-Antonym,

TABLE VIII

BETA WEIGHTS INDICATING RELATIVE CONTRIBUTION OF EACH OF EIGHT CONTENT SUBTESTS TO PREDICTION OF ARITH-RE SCORE AT AGE 14 FOR A FOLLOW-UP GROUP (AGE 34) AND A STATIC GROUP (AGE 14)

Content Subtests	Betas Follow-up ($N = 131$) (Age 34)	Betas Static ($N = 131$) (Age 14)
1. Synonym-Antonym	.20	.19
2. Arithmetic	.20	.28
3. Information	.14	.09
4. Vocabulary	.07	.01
5. Analogies	$-.07$	$-.03$
6. Logical Selection	$-.05$	.01
7. Proverbs	.21	.20
8. Directions	.05	.11
	$R = .66$	$R = .75$

Arithmetic, Information, and Proverbs subtests at both ages 34 and 14 are contributing most to the prediction of the criterion test score (Arith-Re) at age 14. The other four content subtests are contributing very little, if anything, to the prediction of Arith-Re score. The Beta weights show no significant differences between the follow-up group and the static group in amount of contribution to the prediction of the criterion score at age 14.

To summarize, the evidence shows that each of the content subtests does not differ significantly as a measure of intelligence at ages 34 and 14, when validity is estimated by relationship of each content subtest with criterion intelligence test score at age 14. This holds true for both the obtained validities for each of the eight content subtests and the validities with the effect of speed (as measured by "attempts") eliminated. Four of the content subtests—Synonym-Antonym, Arithmetic, Information, and Proverbs—show no significant differences in reliability at both ages 34 and 14. The other four content subtests—Analogies, Vocabulary, Logical Selection, and Directions—are significantly more reliable measures of intelligence at age 34 than at age 14. The content subtests at both age 34 and age 14 which contribute most to the prediction of Arith-Re at age 14 are the same contents having the most consistent reliability at ages 14 and 34—Synonym-Antonym, Arithmetic, Information, and Proverbs.

In conclusion, the findings indicate that in an adult intelligence test standardized against an external criterion of general school achievement as an indicator of intelligence, the contents included in the test do not differ significantly in validity as measures of intelligence at two ages twenty years apart. When the test items, such as the Otis items, are validated against a criterion of general intelligence (in this case, school achievement) and in and of themselves provide good measures of intelligence, the content of the item appears to have little influence on the subject's ability to perform on any specific content either at age 34 or at age 14. Therefore, the hypothesis that the content of adult intelligence tests influences intelligence test score is disproved.

CHAPTER V

SUMMARY AND CONCLUSIONS

THE HYPOTHESIS that has been tested in this investigation is that variation in the content of intelligence tests at the adult level influences estimates of intellectual ability. This hypothesis was formulated to test the findings of several investigations, such as those of Jones and Conrad [11] and Weisenburg, Roe, and McBride [31] in which differential decline among content subtests is evident with increasing age.

A study was made of the relationship between each of several types of content in an adult test of intelligence and a criterion intelligence test score. The intelligence test scores of a group at or near age 14 (the year at which test intelligence was assumed to be near a maximum) were used as the criterion. The performance on subtests of each of several different contents within an intelligence test for the same group at age 34 (a year at which test intelligence is not considered to be at a maximum) was estimated. Differences in the relationships between criterion intelligence test score at age 14 and each content subtest at age 34 were considered measures of the variation in content on adult intelligence tests. In addition, the relationships between each of the content subtests at the same age as criterion intelligence test performance were estimated. Statistically significant differences between the validity coefficients of the content subtests at the age of criterion intelligence test performance and the validity coefficients of the content subtests at the later age were considered as indicative of the degree to which such contents weight an intelligence test score differently for adults as contrasted with children.

Most of the investigations of differential decline among content subtests with age have been based on the mean content

45

scores of cross-sectional samplings of populations assumed to be comparable in intelligence at some critical developmental point. This investigation, however, used both a longitudinal and a cross-sectional approach to estimate the relationships between intelligence test performance for a follow-up group at an early age and their content subtest performance at a later age, as well as the relationship between intelligence test performance and content subtest performance for a group at a static age.

Data from a follow-up group made it possible to determine the validity coefficients of content subtests at age 34 against a criterion intelligence test score at age 14. A group of 131 boys, called the follow-up group, had been tested at or near age 14 with an intelligence test (Arith-Re). This follow-up group had been tested again at or near age 34 with the Otis Self-Administering Test of Mental Ability (Higher Examination: Form B). The items of the Otis subtest, classified according to their content categories, were treated as independent content subtests. The validity of the content subtests at age 34 against the criterion intelligence test score at age 14 was then determined. Knowing the intelligence test performance for the follow-up group at age 14, the relative validity of each of the content subtests as measures of intelligence at age 34 thus was estimated.

Further evidence had to be secured, however, as to the validity of each of the content subtests at age 14 against the criterion of intelligence test score at age 14, to determine whether the content subtests at age 14 were as equally valid as at age 34. To obtain content subtest scores at age 14, a group equivalent in intelligence to the follow-up group at age 14 was given the Otis test at age 14. Then the validity coefficients between content subtests at age 14 and criterion intelligence test score at age 14 could be estimated. The second group of 131 boys, called the static group, was matched with the follow-up group as of age 14 on the basis of age (at or near age 14), amount of schooling (eighth B grade, third month), intelligence test score on Arith-Re at age 14, and scores on the arithmetic and reading tests comprising the Arith-Re test. The static group was given the Otis and the Arith-Re tests at the same time.

The principal findings of the experiment may be summarized as follows:

1. For the follow-up group, there are no significant differences among the relationships between each of the content subtests at 'age 34 and criterion intelligence test score (Arith-Re) at age 14.

For the static group, there are no significant differences among the relationships between each of the content subtests at age 14 and criterion intelligence test score (Arith-Re) at age 14.

There are no statistically significant differences between the validity coefficients of (*a*) the follow-up group—each content subtest at age 34 and Arith-Re at age 14, and (*b*) the static group—each content subtest at age 14 and Arith-Re at age 14.

2. For the follow-up group, the reliability coefficients of each of the content subtests at age 34 indicate that no one content subtest is consistently more reliable than any other. Differences in the reliability coefficients of Vocabulary and three of the contents and in the reliability coefficient of Directions and one content may be attributed to item placement and item opportunity.

For the static group, the reliability coefficients of the content subtests at age 14, however, show significant differences among eight pairs of coefficients. The reliability coefficient of Arithmetic is significantly different from the reliability coefficients of Information, Analogies, and Directions. The reliability coefficient of Proverbs is significantly different from the reliability coefficient of Information, Analogies, Directions, and Logical Selection. The reliability coefficient of Synonym-Antonym is significantly different from that of Analogies.

When the reliability coefficients of each of the content subtests are compared for the follow-up and static groups, there are no significant differences between four of the coefficients: Synonym-Antonym, Arithmetic, Information, and Proverbs. There are significant differences between the follow-up and the static group for the reliability coefficients of Analogies, Vocabulary, Logical Selection, and Directions.

3. For the follow-up group, the validity coefficients corrected

for attenuation are not significantly different from each other in twenty-four pairs of relationships. There are significant differences between four pairs of corrected validity coefficients. The corrected coefficient of Arith-Re and Information is significantly different from three of the coefficients, but this may be attributed to the low reliability of the measure.

For the static group, the validity coefficients corrected for attenuation are not significantly different from each other in twelve pairs of relationships. There are significant differences between sixteen pairs of corrected validity coefficients. The corrected coefficient of Arith-Re and Information is significantly different from six of the corrected coefficients. The corrected coefficient of Arith-Re and Directions is significantly different from five of the corrected coefficients. These differences may be attributed to the low reliability of the measures.

When the validity coefficients corrected for attenuation for the follow-up group are compared with the validity coefficients corrected for attenuation for the static group, there are no significant differences between the following four pairs of the corrected coefficients: Arith-Re and Synonym-Antonym, Arith-Re and Arithmetic, Arith-Re and Vocabulary, Arith-Re and Proverbs. There are significant differences between the corrected coefficients of the two groups in the following four pairs: Arith-Re and Information, Arith-Re and Analogies, Arith-Re and Logical Selection, Arith-Re and Directions.

4. For the follow-up group, when "attempts" (as measure of speed) is partialed out of the validity coefficients, there are no significant differences among the net relationships.

For the static group, when "attempts" is partialed out, there are no significant differences among the net relationships.

There are no statistically significant differences between the net relationships of the follow-up and static groups.

5. The Beta weights of the regression equations for both the follow-up group and the static group indicate that Synonym-Antonym, Arithmetic, Information, and Proverbs subtests at both ages 34 and 14 are contributing most to the prediction of the criterion intelligence test score (Arith-Re) at age 14.

Age 34 was considered as appropriate for testing the relative validity of content subtests as measures of intelligence since differential decline has been shown to be in evidence before this age. The data in this investigation, however, do not allow the conclusion that the content subtests are not significantly different from each other in validity beyond age 34.

According to the findings of the present investigation, each of the content subtests that have been studied was not significantly different in validity from any of the other content subtests, at both ages 34 and 14, against an external criterion of intelligence test score at age 14. Therefore, the hypothesis that variation in the content of intelligence tests at the adult level influences estimates of intellectual ability is untenable.

It is reasonable to assume that the structure of the testing instrument may have influenced the conclusions of other investigations that have shown differential decline among subtests with increasing age. For example, the Army Alpha test, which was the instrument used by Jones and Conrad [11] in arriving at their conclusions, had been constructed by subtests rather than by items. Each subtest had been validated against several criteria: other intelligence tests, officers' ratings, and school achievement. Although the content subtests show high correlation with these criteria,[1] nevertheless the ability of each item in each subtest to appraise intelligence is not indicated.

The committee working on the construction of this test accepted the principle that the test as a whole should measure many aspects of intelligence. The guiding principles determining the choice of content subtests were content validity, nondependence upon schooling, interest and appeal, and factors concerned with problems of administration.[2] The difficulty of each item was rated in many cases by judgment of the committee, and harder items "of an abstract type"[3] were added at the end of the subtest to make up the required number of items

---

[1] R. M. Yerkes (ed.), *Psychological Examining in the United States Army*, pp. 337, 432–33, 781. Memoirs of the National Academy of Science, Vol. 15. Government Printing Office, Washington, D. C., 1921.

[2] *Ibid.*, pp. 299 ff.

[3] *Ibid.*, p. 340.

where needed. The findings of the present investigation imply that unless each item is chosen to appraise intelligence against some definitive criterion of intelligence, items which may not be especially adequate as measures of intelligence over a wide age range may be operating to depress content subtest scores. Item difficulty of itself as determined by the percent passing each item may not be sufficient indication that the item is adequate in appraising intelligence unless the item discriminates between known groups. Even on the Wechsler-Bellevue test, the content subtests were validated as a whole and therefore Wechsler [30] found that some subtests hold up with age much better than others. That the items in the Alpha subtests may not have been equally adequate in appraising the intelligence of the older groups in the Jones and Conrad population may have contributed to differential decline among the content subtests.

On the Otis test, which was used in this investigation to test differential decline among the items classified into content subtests, each item had been chosen by Otis for its ability to select bright students as compared with dull students. This method of item validation makes each item a good measure of intelligence by itself, regardless of the content of the item. When the items are grouped into content subtests, they would be expected to show no significant differences in validity against an external criterion of intelligence. But if content were operative in influencing test score at an age at which differential decline among content subtests has been shown, then the relationships between each of the content subtests at age 34 and the external criterion at age 14 would have shown significant differences. Since there were no differences, differential decline cannot be attributed to variation in content at this age level.

That some contents are more intellectual than others and therefore decline more rapidly has been suggested by Jones and Conrad.[4] They state that in Test 7 (Analogies) of the Alpha test the cause of the decline lies in the intellectual difficulty of

[4] H. E. Jones and H. S. Conrad, *The Growth and Decline of Intelligence.* Genetic Psychology Monographs, Vol. 13, No. 3, March, 1933, p. 257.

the task and not in factors associated with speed of reading or in the motivation of rapid work. Weisenburg, Roe, and Mc-Bride also note this fairly rapid decline in Analogies as compared with other tests in their battery, even though its correlation with Stanford-Binet is .72.[5] Apparently, then, Analogies is a fairly adequate measure of intelligence when it is validated against as excellent an external criterion as Stanford-Binet. Decrement in mean score with age on Analogies could not be attributed to any inherent inadequacy of the test itself with increasing age. Thus factors other than content must be sought as contributing to the decline. Jones and Conrad have maintained that the tests showing most rapid decline are Test 7 (Analogies), Test 3 ("Common Sense"), and Test 6 (Numerical Completions). They state: "These tests may perhaps be considered at least on *a priori* grounds, to be the best in the Alpha for the measurement of basic intelligence, i. e., to be the most free from the accumulative effects of differential experience."[6]

One would first have to establish a basis or a criterion of intellectuality before it could be asserted that tests of such content are more intellectual as indicated by higher relationship with an acceptable criterion of intellectuality than the other content subtests of the Alpha test. Yet this investigation, using as a criterion of intellectual status a test score at or near a maturation point of test intelligence, shows that none of the content subtests appear to be better measures of intelligence than any other.

The assertion of Jones and Conrad that those contents which are not derived from school experience are more intellectual than the contents dependent upon schooling requires further definition of intellectuality. Amount of intelligence, or degree of intelligence, has of necessity been estimated by testing instruments which in themselves are fallible. Amount of schooling has been shown to relate closely to intelligence test score. It is known that the correlation between acceptable tests of intel-

---

[5] T. Weisenburg, A. Roe, and K. E. McBride, *Adult Intelligence*, p. 89. The Commonwealth Fund, New York, 1936.

[6] Jones and Conrad, *op. cit.*, p. 253.

ligence and schooling will be approximately .7 or higher. In spite of the fact that one of the criteria of test selection on the Alpha test included non-dependence on schooling, it has never been possible to construct a test of the Army Alpha form that did not correlate highly with schooling. Yerkes[7] makes the following observation: "The better educated the group, the better its record on the intelligence examinations; or, equally truly, the better the intelligence rating a group can make, the more education it has obtained." Lorge [17] also points out that among groups equated on intelligence test score in adolescence, there was a greater increment in test score at a later age for those with the greater amount of schooling. In addition, the results on Alpha give no indication that the tests differ greatly in the extent to which schooling influences the results.

Thus amount of schooling must relate equally well to each of the content subtests on the Alpha test. Census reports have established that the average years of schooling in the United States for the total population diminishes with successively older age groups. Insofar as older people have less schooling, and insofar as intelligence tests have a high correlation with schooling, it follows that the older the subjects, the poorer will be their performance on tests of intelligence. Actually, no content, as far as can be determined, is free from the effects of schooling, and therefore no content can be called more intellectual than any other until some other criterion of intellectuality is set up. That experience and vocational pursuit may counteract lower scores on some content subtests of older populations may be factors contributing to differential decline.

Inasmuch as this investigation has proved that there are age differences between the reliability coefficients of various contents, content reliability must be considered a factor contributing to differential decline with age. Two notions of reliability must be taken into account. The first concept is that of the statistically significant differences between the reliability coefficients of the several content subtests at different age levels. The second concept is that of the reliability of each

[7] Yerkes, *op. cit.*, p. 764.

item as measuring the specific content ability which it purports to measure.

It is interesting to note that the content subtests of the Otis test in this investigation showing the most consistent reliability at ages 14 and 34 are similar in type to the contents of the Alpha test which Jones and Conrad found to show least decline with age. In the present investigation, Synonym-Antonym, Arithmetic, and Information content show no significant differences between their reliability coefficients at ages 14 and 34. Jones and Conrad found that Opposites (which may be assumed to measure the same abilities as Synonym-Antonym), Arithmetic, and Information showed least decline with age. This fact is suggestive of the conclusion that contents having consistent reliability are better measures for comparing the intelligence of groups over a wide age range than contents showing significant differences in reliability for different age groups. The Analogies, Directions, and Logical Selection contents in this investigation show significant differences in their reliability coefficients between ages 14 and 34. Jones and Conrad have shown that Analogies, Directions, and "Common Sense" (which for purposes of comparison may be considered similar to Logical Selection) show greatest decline with age. Perhaps the differences in the reliabilities of these subtests are operative in creating the decline for the various age groups studied. The conclusion would follow, therefore, that when intelligence tests are constructed for appraising groups over a wide age range, only those contents should be included in the test that show equivalent reliability for appraising different age groups; otherwise the inclusion of contents showing age differences in reliability will penalize the age group for which the contents are known to be less reliable measures. Before the assumption can be made that the eight subtests of Alpha are equally reliable measures for a population aged 10 to 60 years, the reliability of the contents would have to be estimated for decade groups from 10 to 60 years.

The second concept to be considered is that of the reliability of each item as a measure of the specific content it is supposed to measure. On the Alpha test, after the content subtests had been chosen according to the criteria set up by the committee, the items assumed to be indicative of such contents were constructed. What the items were actually appraising depended on the judgment of the individual choosing the item. While it may be assumed, therefore, that each item assigned to Arithmetic, Opposites, etc., was actually testing ability on that specific content, even the committee points out that on the Information test, for example, the first ten items seem to depend more on reading ability than on Information.[8] What is noted by Jones and Conrad as rise in information ability with age may actually indicate rise in reading ability with age. Norris [22] shows that some abilities, such as reading, which are dependent on experience, continue to develop beyond school years. Therefore, to assume that Information rather than some other ability is being appraised raises the question of how effectively each item is testing the specific content. For example, as mentioned in Chapter II, page 21, Otis states that the items in his test were chosen for their ability to appraise intelligence, not for their ability to measure any specific content. Nevertheless, that each item does measure some specific content is indicated by the high percentage of agreement among the judges who classified the items into content categories. The issue again resolves itself into the problem of choice of each item in the test as a good measure of intelligence rather than choice of each item as a measure of specific content. Each item is saturated with many abilities which are included in the appraisal of intelligence, and to assume that the contents themselves are the factors contributing to differential decline has been shown to be untenable, since the contents consist of items which are measuring simultaneously many aspects of intelligence.

A further issue to consider as contributory to differential decline among contents is that of motivation. The committee reporting on Army Alpha recognized this fact, for they suggest that the test may be improved by more effective combinations of Alpha with other tests of a somewhat different nature, per-

8 Yerkes, *op. cit.*, p. 341.

haps with "omnibus" tests involving more frequent change of problem.[9] When a test is set up like the Army Alpha test, in which the subjects are required to perform on a specific kind of content for successive items, a negative reaction toward school type or unfamiliar subject matter may occur in the older adult. Consequently, some content subtests which are distasteful or less challenging to the older adult will appear to be more difficult simply because the subject does not exert as much effort on such content as on content with which he is more familiar. The younger adult who has less firmly established patterns of rejection will attempt all the items, regardless of their novelty or unfamiliarity. Jones and Conrad maintain that age was of little importance in determining incentive, but their conclusions are based on the lack of differences between home-tested cases which were highly motivated and group-tested cases in which motivation was less strictly controllable.[10] However, the motivation for different age groups may still be operative when items of a specific content are presented to the subject in consecutive order, as suggested by Yerkes. In the present investigation, in which the items are presented in "omnibus" fashion, the follow-up group at age 34 and the static group at age 14 attempt approximately the same number of items in each content subtest, even though the static group lacking the experience and added schooling of the follow-up group gets fewer items correct in each category. This is suggestive of further investigation.

Before differential decline among content subtests can be asserted, some account must be taken of previous intellectual status at a criterion point in test intelligence. When extent of vocabulary was used as the index of previous intellectual functioning, significant decline in some abilities was found after age 50 by Babcock [1], and after age 60 by Gilbert [9]. Among other investigators, Jones and Conrad [11] and Wechsler [30] have noted differential decline among content subtests beginning as early as age 20, although some contents maintain their

9 Yerkes, *op. cit.*, p. 345.
10 Jones and Conrad, *op. cit.*, p. 255.

development and even continue to increase after this age. Wechsler recognized this fact and consequently standardized his test on different age groups, so that norms could be established for different age levels. The factorial analyses by Balinsky [2] and Lorge [16] of Wechsler's standardization data have shown different factorial composition at ages 9 and 12 as compared with ages 25–29 and 35–40. That different mental processes may be required in the test performance of young age groups as compared with age groups after age 25 is evident from the Balinsky and Lorge findings. Even though the same test score is attained by both young and older subjects, a different mental process may be employed by the different age groups to achieve the same score.

This investigation has shown that when intellectual status is known for a group at age 14, subtests of different contents at age 34 are not significantly different in validity as measures of intelligence.

BIBLIOGRAPHY

1. BABCOCK, HARRIET. *An Experiment in the Measurement of Mental Deterioration.* Archives of Psychology, Vol. 18, No. 117. Columbia University, August, 1930.
2. BALINSKY, BENJAMIN. *An Analysis of the Mental Factors of Various Age Groups from Nine to Sixty.* Genetic Psychology Monographs, Vol. 23, February, 1941, pp. 191–234. The Journal Press, Provincetown, Mass., 1941.
3. BINGHAM, WALTER VAN DYKE. *Aptitudes and Aptitude Testing.* Harper & Brothers, New York, 1937.
4. BRODY, M. B. "A Survey of the Results of Intelligence Tests in Psychosis." *British Journal of Medical Psychology,* Vol. 19 (Part 2), 1942, pp. 215–257.
5. CATTELL, RAYMOND B. "The Measurement of Adult Intelligence." *Psychological Bulletin,* Vol. 40, No. 3, March, 1943, pp. 153–193.
6. CHRISTIAN, ALICE M. and PATERSON, DONALD G. "Growth of Vocabulary in Later Maturity." *Journal of Psychology,* Vol. I, January, 1936, pp. 167–169.
7. FREEMAN, FRANK N. and FLORY, CHARLES D. *Growth in Intellectual Ability as Measured by Repeated Tests.* Society for Research in Child Development, Vol. II, No. 2. National Research Council, Washington, D. C., 1937.
8. GILBERT, JEANNE G. "Discussion—Old Age and Aging: The Evolution and Mental Status as a Function of the Mental Test." *American Journal of Orthopsychiatry,* Vol. 10, January, 1940.
9. GILBERT, JEANNE G. *Mental Efficiency in Senescence.* Archives of Psychology, No. 188. Columbia University, July, 1935.
10. HOLLINGWORTH, HARRY LEVI. *Mental Growth and Decline: A Survey of Developmental Psychology.* Appleton & Co., New York, 1927.
11. JONES, HAROLD E. and CONRAD, HERBERT S. *The Growth and Decline of Intelligence: A Study of a Homogeneous Group Between the Ages of Ten and Sixty.* Genetic Psychology Monographs, Vol. 13, No. 3, March, 1933, pp. 223–298. Clark University, Worcester, Mass., 1933.
12. KUDER, G. F. and RICHARDSON, M. W. "The Theory of the Estimation of Test Reliability." *Psychometrika,* Vol. 2, No. 3, September, 1937, pp. 151–160.
13. LORGE, IRVING. "Intellectual Changes During Maturity and Old Age."

Review of Educational Research, Vol. 11, No. 5, December, 1941, pp. 553–561.

14. LORGE, IRVING. "Intellectual Changes During Maturity and Old Age." *Review of Educational Research,* Vol. 14, No. 5, December, 1944, pp. 438–445.

15. LORGE, IRVING. "Retests After Ten Years." *Journal of Educational Psychology,* Vol. 25, No. 2, February, 1934, pp. 136–141.

16. LORGE, IRVING. "Review of 'The Measurement of Adult Intelligence' by D. Wechsler." *Journal of Consulting Psychology.* Vol. 7, January–December, 1943, pp. 167–168.

17. LORGE, IRVING. "Schooling Makes a Difference." *Teachers College Record,* Vol. 46, No. 8, May, 1945, pp. 483–492.

18. LORGE, IRVING. "The Influence of the Test Upon the Nature of Mental Decline as a Function of Age." *Journal of Educational Psychology,* Vol. 27, No. 1, January, 1936, pp. 100–110.

19. LORGE, IRVING and BLAU, RAPHAEL. "Reading Comprehension of Adults." *Teachers College Record,* Vol. 43, No. 3, October 1941–May, 1942, pp. 189–198.

20. MILES, WALTER R. "Age and Human Ability." *Psychological Review,* Vol. 40, No. 2, March, 1933, pp. 99–123.

21. MILES, WALTER R. "Psychological Aspects of Ageing," in *Problems of Ageing: Biological and Medical Aspects* (E. V. Cowdry, ed.). Williams and Wilkins Co., Baltimore, 1939.

22. NORRIS, K. E. *The Three R's and the Adult Worker.* McGill University, Montreal, 1940.

23. OTIS, ARTHUR S. *Otis Self-Administering Tests of Mental Ability. Manual of Directions and Key (Revised).* World Book Co., Yonkers, N. Y., 1928.

24. PINTNER, RUDOLF. *Intelligence Testing.* Henry Holt and Co., (new ed.), New York, 1931.

25. SORENSON, HERBERT. "Mental Ability Over a Wide Range of Adult Ages." *Journal of Applied Psychology,* Vol. 17, 1933, pp. 729–741.

26. TERMAN, LEWIS M. and MERRILL, MAUD A. *Measuring Intelligence.* Houghton Mifflin Co., Boston, 1937.

27. THORNDIKE, EDWARD LEE AND OTHERS. *Prediction of Vocational Success.* The Commonwealth Fund, New York, 1934.

28. THORNDIKE, ROBERT L. "The Effect of the Interval Between Test and Retest on the Constancy of the I.Q. "*Journal of Educational Psychology,* Vol. 24, No. 1, January, 1933, pp. 543–549.

29. TOOPS, HERBERT ANDERSON. *Tests for Vocational Guidance of Children Thirteen to Sixteen.* Contributions to Education, No. 136. Bureau of Publications, Teachers College, Columbia University, New York, 1923.

30. WECHSLER, DAVID. *The Measurement of Adult Intelligence.* Williams and Wilkins Co., Baltimore, 1941.

31. WEISENBURG, THEODORE, ROE, ANNE, and McBRIDE, KATHERINE E. *Adult Intelligence; a Psychological Study of Test Performances.* The Commonwealth Fund, New York, 1936.

32. YERKES, ROBERT MEARNS (ed.). *Psychological Examining in the United States Army.* Memoirs of the National Academy of Science, Vol. 15. Government Printing Office, Washington, D. C., 1921.

33. YOAKUM, CLARENCE STONE and YERKES, ROBERT MEARNS. *Army Mental Tests.* Henry Holt and Co., New York, 1920.